Learn about Angular Framework

The Angular framework is a JavaScript-based web application framework that is used for building single-page web applications. The framework is also used for creating reusable components that can be used in other web applications.

The book covers the following:

Chapter 1: Introduction to Angular

Introduction to Angular framework

Angular architecture overview

Setting up the Angular development environment

Creating your first Angular application

Exploring Angular project structure

Chapter 2: Components and Templates in Angular

Understanding components and templates in Angular

Creating and using components in Angular

Data binding and interpolation in Angular

Directives in Angular (structural and attribute)

Template syntax and best practices in Angular

Chapter 3: Services and Dependency Injection in Angular

Introduction to services and dependency injection in Angular

Creating and using services in Angular

Understanding providers and injectors in Angular

Hierarchical injectors and dependency resolution in Angular

Advanced dependency injection techniques in Angular

Chapter 4: Routing and Navigation in Angular

Introduction to Angular routing

Configuring routes and route parameters in Angular

Route guards for authentication and authorization in Angular

Lazy loading and preloading strategies in Angular

Implementing nested routes and child routers in Angular

Chapter 5: Forms and Validation in Angular

Angular forms overview

Template-driven forms in Angular

Reactive forms and form validation in Angular

Working with form controls and form groups in Angular

Custom form validators and error handling in Angular

Chapter 6: HTTP Communication in Angular

Introduction to HTTP module in Angular

Sending GET, POST, PUT, and DELETE requests in Angular

Handling request and response using observables in Angular

Interceptors and error handling in HTTP requests in Angular

Caching and authentication with HTTP requests in Angular

Chapter 7: State Management with NgRx in Angular

Understanding state management and NgRx in Angular

Setting up NgRx in Angular application

Actions, reducers, and selectors in Angular

Managing side effects with NgRx effects in Angular

Best practices and advanced concepts in NgRx in Angular

Chapter 8: Angular and RESTful APIs

Consuming RESTful APIs in Angular

Working with RESTful API endpoints in Angular

Implementing pagination and filtering in Angular

Error handling and retry strategies in Angular

Testing Angular services and HTTP requests

Chapter 9: Unit Testing in Angular

Introduction to unit testing in Angular

Setting up testing environment with Karma and Jasmine in Angular

Writing unit tests for components and services in Angular

Testing asynchronous code and observables in Angular

Code coverage and best practices for testing in Angular

Chapter 10: Advanced Component Techniques in Angular

Dynamic component creation and rendering in Angular

Component communication using input/output properties in Angular

ViewChild and ContentChild decorators in Angular

Change detection strategies and performance optimization in Angular

Creating reusable components and component libraries in Angular

Chapter 11: Internationalization and Localization in Angular

Introduction to internationalization and localization in Angular

Configuring multiple languages in Angular

Implementing translations with ngx-translate in Angular

Date, number, and currency formatting in Angular

Best practices for building multilingual applications in Angular

Chapter 12: Deployment and Optimization in Angular

Building and packaging Angular application for production

Performance optimization techniques in Angular

Tree shaking and code minification in Angular

Lazy loading and optimizing bundle size in Angular

Continuous integration and deployment strategies in Angular

Chapter 1: Introduction to Angular

The Angular framework is a JavaScript-based web application framework that is used for building single-page web applications. The framework is also used for creating reusable components that can be used in other web applications. The Angular framework is a tool that helps developers to create web applications that are fast, responsive, and easy to maintain.

Introduction to Angular framework

Angular is a JavaScript framework for building web applications and SPAs (Single Page Applications). It is a complete rewrite of the AngularJS framework. Angular is a TypeScript-based open-source front-end web application platform led by the Angular Team at Google and by a community of individuals and corporations. Angular is a platform for building mobile and desktop web applications.

The Angular framework is one of the most popular front-end web development frameworks, and is used by millions of developers all over the world.

The Angular framework is open source, and is maintained by Google.

The Angular framework is based on the Model-View-Controller (MVC) design pattern, and is composed of three main components:

- The Model, which represents the data to be displayed in the view.
- The View, which is the HTML template that is rendered in the browser.
- The Controller, which is the TypeScript code that interacts with the model and the view.

The Angular framework can be used to build web applications for both desktop and mobile devices. The Angular framework is also used to build native mobile apps using the Angular Native library.

The Angular framework is one of the most popular front-end web development frameworks, and is used by millions of developers all over the world.

Angular architecture overview

The Angular architecture is based on a hierarchy of components, with each component having a specific purpose. The top-level component is the root component, which contains all the other components. The root component is the only component that is required for an Angular application. Each component has a template, which is the HTML that defines the component's user interface. The template is compiled into a component factory, which is used to create instances of the component. The component instances are then added to the DOM, where they are rendered.

Setting up the Angular development environment

Assuming you have Node.js installed, you can create a new Angular project by using the Angular CLI tool.

First, install the Angular CLI tool using the following command:

npm install -g @angular/cli

Next, create a new project using the following command:

ng new my-app

This will create a new directory called my-app that contains the initial project files.

Next, you need to install the project dependencies. Change into the new project directory and use the following command:

npm install

Once the dependencies have been installed, you can launch the development server using the following command:

ng serve

The development server will be running on http://localhost:4200/.

Creating your first Angular application

There are a few different ways to create your first Angular application. One way is to use the Angular CLI, which is a command line interface tool that can be used to create and manage Angular projects.

Another way is to create your own Angular application using a text editor and a web server. This approach is more manual, but can be a good way to get started and learn more about how Angular works.

To use the Angular CLI to create a new Angular project, open a terminal window and type the following command:

ng new my-app

This will create a new directory called my-app that contains all the files needed for a basic Angular application.

Once the project is created, you can open it in your text editor and start adding code. The main file you'll work with is the src/app/app.component.ts file, which contains the code for the root component of your application.

To run your application, you'll need to install the Angular CLI and use the ng serve command. This will start a web server that will serve your application on http://localhost:4200.

You can also use the Angular CLI to generate new components, services, and other files. For more information, see the Angular CLI documentation.

Exploring Angular project structure

The Angular project structure is based on the Model View Controller (MVC) design pattern. The project is divided into three parts: the model, the view, and the controller.

The model is responsible for storing data and business logic. The view is responsible for displaying data to the user. The controller is responsible for handling user input and updating the model and view.

The project structure is designed to make it easy to add new features and make changes to existing features. The project is modular, so each part of the project can be updated independently.

Chapter 2: Components and Templates in Angular

Understanding components and templates in Angular

Components are the building blocks of an Angular application. They are self-contained and reusable units of functionality. Angular components are typically written in TypeScript, and have an HTML template that defines the component's user interface.

Templates are the HTML files that define the component's user interface. They are typically written in HTML, but can also include other template languages such as Angular's own template language, or Microsoft's ClearScript.

When a component is instantiated, Angular creates a new instance of the component's template. This template is then used to render the component's user interface. The template can access the component's data and methods, and can also be used to handle user input events.

Components are the basic building blocks of an Angular application. They are self-contained and reusable units of code that can be used to build larger applications. Angular components are typically written in TypeScript and have an HTML template that defines the component's user interface.

Creating a component in Angular is a two-step process. First, you need to write the TypeScript code for the component. Second, you need to define the HTML template for the component.

The TypeScript code for a component is typically written in a file with a ".ts" extension. The HTML template for a component is typically written in a file with a ".html" extension.

When you create a new component in Angular, you need to register it with the application. This is done in the "app.module.ts" file.

Once a component is registered with the application, you can use it in other parts of the application. For example, you can use it in another component's template.

When using a component in another component's template, you need to use the correct Angular syntax. This is typically done with a "selector" attribute. The value of the selector attribute is the name of the component.

Angular also provides a number of other attributes that can be used when using components. For example, the "inputs" attribute can be used to pass data into a component. The "outputs" attribute can be used to get data out of a component.

Components can also be nested inside of other components. This is a powerful way to build large applications from small, reusable pieces.

Data binding and interpolation in Angular

Data binding is the process of connecting a data source to a UI element. This connection allows the data to flow both ways, from the data source to the UI element and from the UI element back to the data source.

Interpolation is a type of data binding that allows you to insert the value of a data source into a UI element. This is done by using double curly braces around the data source name, which tells Angular to insert the value of the data source into that spot in the template.

A directive is a class with a @Directive decorator. A structural directive changes the DOM layout by adding and removing DOM elements. An attribute directive changes the appearance or behavior of an element, component, or another directive.

There are three kinds of directives in Angular:

Component directives

Structural directives

Attribute directives

Component Directives

A component directive is created with the @Component decorator. A component is a directive with a template. A component has its own view.

Structural Directives

A structural directive changes the DOM layout by adding and removing DOM elements.

Attribute Directives

An attribute directive changes the appearance or behavior of an element, component, or another directive.

Template syntax and best practices in Angular

When creating Angular templates, there are a few best practices to keep in mind in order to keep your code clean and maintainable.

1. Use the correct template syntax for your version of Angular. Angular 2+ uses a different template syntax than Angular 1.x, so be sure to use the correct syntax for your version.

2. Keep your templates simple. Avoid using too many directives or complex expressions in your templates. This will make your code more difficult to read and maintain.

3. Use a consistent indentation style for your templates. This will make your code more readable and easier to debug.

4. Use a template linter tool to check your code for errors. This will help you catch errors early and prevent them from causing problems in your application.

Chapter 3: Services and Dependency Injection in Angular

Introduction to services and dependency injection in Angular

In Angular, a service is an injectable class with a defined purpose. Services are typically used for cross-component functionality, such as retrieving data from an API or logging in a user. Angular provides a built-in dependency injection system that makes it easy to inject services into components.

When a service is injected into a component, it is available to the component and its child components. Services can also be injected into other services. This is known as dependency injection.

Dependency injection is a powerful technique for managing dependencies between classes. By injecting a service into a component, we can be sure that the component will always have access to the latest version of the service. This is especially important when services are being updated frequently.

Injecting a service into a component is simple. First, we need to add the service to the component's providers array. Then, we can inject the service into the component's constructor:

```
constructor(private myService: MyService) { }
```

Once the service is injected, we can access it from anywhere within the component:

```
this.myService.getData();
```

Injecting a service into another service is just as easy. We simply need to add the service to the providers array of the injector service:

```
constructor(private myService: MyService, private injector: Injector) { }
```

Then, we can inject the service into the constructor of the other service:

```
constructor(private myService: MyService, private injector: Injector) { this.otherService = this.injector.get(OtherService); }
```

This technique is especially useful when we need to inject a service into a service that is already being injected into a component. By injecting the service into the injector service, we can be sure that the service will always be available to the component.

In summary, services and dependency injection are powerful tools for managing dependencies between classes in Angular. Services can be injected into components and other services, making them available anywhere within the application. This is a powerful technique for ensuring that components always have access to the latest version of a service.

Creating and using services in Angular

In Angular, a service is a class with a defined purpose. This purpose can be anything, from retrieving data from an API, to logging user activity, to managing state. Angular services are singletons, meaning that there is only one instance of a service in an Angular application.

Angular services are injected into classes using the dependency injection (DI) system. This is a powerful system that helps make Angular applications modular and extensible. When a service is injected into a class, the service becomes a property of that class.

There are two ways to create services in Angular:

1. Use the Angular CLI to generate a service.

2. Create a service manually.

To generate a service using the Angular CLI, you can use the following command:

ng generate service my-service

This will create a file called my-service.service.ts in the src/app directory. The contents of this file will look like this:

import { Injectable } from '@angular/core';

@Injectable({

providedIn: 'root'

})

export class MyService {

constructor() { }

```
}
```

The @Injectable decorator is required for all services. The providedIn property tells Angular where to inject the service. In this case, the service will be injected into the root of the application, meaning it will be available everywhere.

If you need to inject a service into a specific component, you can use the following syntax:

```
@Injectable({

providedIn: 'MyComponent'

})
```

This will make the service available only in the MyComponent component.

To create a service manually, you simply create a class with the desired functionality. For example, if you wanted to create a service that retrieved data from an API, you might do something like this:

```
import { Injectable } from '@angular/core';
```

```
import { HttpClient } from
'@angular/common/http';

@Injectable({

providedIn: 'root'

})

export class MyService {

constructor(private http: HttpClient) { }

getData() {

return this.http.get('https://my-api.com/data');

}

}
```

In this example, the MyService class is injecting the
HttpClient service. This is a built-in Angular
service that allows you to make HTTP requests.

Once you have created a service, you can inject it
into any class that needs it. For example, if you
have a component that needs to use the MyService
service, you would inject it like this:

```
import { Component } from '@angular/core';
```

```
import { MyService } from './my.service';

@Component({

selector: 'app-my-component',

templateUrl: './my-component.component.html',

styleUrls: ['./my-component.component.css']

})

export class MyComponentComponent {

constructor(private myService: MyService) { }

ngOnInit() {

this.myService.getData().subscribe(data => {

// do something with the data

});

}

}
```

In this example, the MyComponentComponent is injecting the MyService service. It is then using the MyService service to make an HTTP request to an API.

Services are a powerful way to share data and functionality between different parts of an Angular application. By using the dependency injection system, Angular makes it easy to inject services into components.

Understanding providers and injectors in Angular

In Angular, providers and injectors are used to manage dependencies between services and components. Providers provide services to components, and injectors inject those services into components.

Injectors are used to resolve dependencies between services and components. They are created by the Angular injector service, and they can be used to resolve dependencies for services and components.

Providers provide services to components. They are registered with the Angular provider service, and they can be used to provide services to components.

Hierarchical injectors and dependency resolution in Angular

Angular's hierarchical injector system is one of the most powerful features of the framework. It allows developers to declaratively specify dependencies between services, and have those dependencies automatically resolved and injected by the injector.

The hierarchical injector system is also used for dependency resolution in Angular. When a component or service is requested, the injector will first look for a provider registered with the same key in the current injector scope. If no provider is found, the injector will walk up the scope hierarchy, looking for providers registered in the parent scope. This continues until a provider is found or the root injector scope is reached.

This system allows Angular to automatically resolve dependencies between services, and is also used for dependency injection into components and services.

In Angular, dependency injection is a powerful technique that is often used in conjunction with services to modularize and reuse code. There are a number of ways to do dependency injection, but some of the more advanced techniques include:

1. Inline Annotation:

With inline annotation, dependencies are declared directly on the service class. This is a convenient way to declare dependencies, but it can make the code difficult to read and maintain.

2. Decorator Pattern:

With the decorator pattern, dependencies are declared using a decorator function. This technique is more flexible than inline annotation and can make the code easier to read and maintain.

3. Factory Pattern:

With the factory pattern, dependencies are declared using a factory function. This technique is more flexible than the decorator pattern and can make the code easier to read and maintain.

4. Service Locator Pattern:

With the service locator pattern, dependencies are declared using a service locator object. This technique is more flexible than the factory pattern and can make the code easier to read and maintain.

Chapter 4: Routing and Navigation in Angular

Introduction to Angular routing

Angular routing is a powerful feature that allows developers to build Single Page Applications (SPAs) with rich client-side functionality. Angular's router is different from traditional server-side routing in that it allows for a declarative, component-based approach to client-side routing. This means that instead of having to define routes in a central location (like a server-side application), routes are defined directly in the component files.

This approach has a number of benefits, including:

1. It makes it easy to see which components are associated with which routes.

2. It makes it easy to change the URL without having to change the code in multiple places.

3. It makes it easy to unit test the routing logic.

4. It makes it easy to lazy-load components, which can improve the performance of the application.

To use Angular routing, you need to include the router library in your project. The router library is available as a package on npm, so you can install it using the following command:

npm install @angular/router

Once the router library is installed, you can import it into your application using the following code:

import { RouterModule } from '@angular/router';

The router library provides a number of different directives that can be used to define routes in your application. The most commonly used directive is the routerLink directive. The routerLink directive can be used to generate links to different parts of the application. For example, the following code would generate a link to the home page:

<a routerLink="/">Home</a>

The routerLink directive can also be used to generate links to child routes. For example, if your application has a route for /products/:id, you can use the routerLink directive to generate a link to that route by providing the id parameter:

```
<a routerLink="/products/123">Product
Details</a>
```

If you want to generate a link to a route that has query parameters, you can use the queryParams directive. For example, if your application has a route for /search?q=:query, you can use the queryParams directive to generate a link to that route by providing the query parameter:

```
<a routerLink="/search" [queryParams]="{ q:
'query' }">Search</a>
```

The routerLink directive can also be used to generate links to relative routes. For example, if your application has a route for /products/:id, and the current URL is /products/123, you can use the routerLink directive to generate a link to the route for /products/:id without specifying the id parameter:

```
<a routerLink="../products/123">Product
Details</a>
```

The routerLink directive can also be used to generate links to absolute routes. For example, if your application has a route for /products/:id, and the current URL is /products/123, you can use the routerLink directive to generate a link to the route for /products without specifying the id parameter:

```
<a routerLink="/products">Products</a>
```

In addition to the routerLink directive, the router library also provides the routerLinkActive directive. The routerLinkActive directive can be used to add a class to an element when the route is active. For example, the following code would add the active class to the element when the route is /products:

```
<a routerLink="/products"
routerLinkActive="active">Products</a>
```

The routerLinkActive directive can also be used to add a class to an element when the route is active and the URL contains a specific query parameter. For example, the following code would add the active class to the element when the route is /search and the q query parameter is present in the URL:

```
<a routerLink="/search"
routerLinkActive="active" [queryParams]="{ q:
'query' }">Search</a>
```

The router library also provides the routerOutlet directive. The routerOutlet directive is used to render the content of a route. For example, the following code would render the content of the route for /products:

```
<router-outlet></router-outlet>
```

The routerOutlet directive can also be used to render the content of a child route. For example, if your application has a route for /products/:id, you can use the routerOutlet directive to render the content of that route by providing the id parameter:

```
<router-outlet [routeParams]="{ id: '123' }"></router-outlet>
```

In addition to the routerOutlet directive, the router library also provides the routerLinkActiveOptions directive. The routerLinkActiveOptions directive can be used to configure the routerLinkActive directive. For example, the following code would add the active class to the element when the route is /products and the exact match is true:

```
<a routerLink="/products"
routerLinkActive="active"
[routerLinkActiveOptions]="{ exact: true
}">Products</a>
```

The router library also provides the routerLinkWithHref directive. The routerLinkWithHref directive can be used to generate links to routes that contain non-standard characters in the URL. For example, the following code would generate a link to the route for /products/:id:

```
<a routerLinkWithHref="/products/:id">Product
Details</a>
```

The routerLinkWithHref directive can also be used to generate links to child routes. For example, if your application has a route for /products/:id, you can use the routerLinkWithHref directive to generate a link to that route by providing the id parameter:

```
<a routerLinkWithHref="/products/:id"
[routeParams]="{ id: '123' }">Product Details</a>
```

The router library also provides the routerLinkActiveOptions directive. The routerLinkActiveOptions directive can be used to configure the routerLinkActive directive. For example, the following code would add the active class to the element when the route is /products and the exact match is true:

```
<a routerLink="/products"
routerLinkActive="active"
[routerLinkActiveOptions]="{ exact: true
}">Products</a>
```

The router library also provides the routerLinkWithHref directive. The routerLinkWithHref directive can be used to generate links to routes that contain non-standard characters in the URL. For example, the following code would generate a link to the route for /products/:id:

```
<a routerLinkWithHref="/products/:id">Product
Details</a>
```

The routerLinkWithHref directive can also be used to generate links to child routes. For example, if your application has a route for /products/:id, you can use the routerLinkWithHref directive to generate a link to that route by providing the id parameter:

```
<a routerLinkWithHref="/products/:id"
[routeParams]="{ id: '123' }">Product Details</a>
```

The router library also provides the routerLinkActiveOptions directive. The routerLinkActiveOptions directive can be used to configure the routerLinkActive directive. For example, the following code would add the active class to the element when the route is /products and the exact match is true:

```
<a routerLink="/products"
routerLinkActive="active"
[routerLinkActiveOptions]="{ exact: true }">Products</a>
```

Configuring routes and route parameters in Angular

Configuring routes and route parameters in Angular is done in the file called "routes.ts". The "routes.ts" file contains the configuration for the router and the routes. The router is responsible for mapping URLs to components. The routes are responsible for mapping URLs to the corresponding component templates.

In the "routes.ts" file, there is an array of route objects. Each route object has a "path" property and a "component" property. The "path" property specifies the URL that the route corresponds to. The "component" property specifies the component that the route renders.

Route parameters are specified in the "path" property of the route object. The syntax for specifying a route parameter is: ":parameterName". For example, if the "path" property is "/user/:id", then the "id" route parameter will be populated with the value of the "id" URL parameter.

To access the value of a route parameter, you use the "params" property of the "ActivatedRoute" object. The "params" property is an observable, so you can subscribe to it in order to get the current value of the route parameters.

Here is an example of how to subscribe to the "params" observable in order to get the value of the "id" route parameter:

```
this.route.params.subscribe(params => {
```

```
let id = params['id'];

// ...

});
```

Route guards for authentication and authorization in Angular

Route guards are used to protect routes from unauthorized access. They can be used to check if a user is logged in, has the necessary permissions, or is allowed to access a route. Guards can be used to prevent users from accessing a route, or to redirect them to a different route.

There are different types of route guards, including:

CanActivate: This guard is used to prevent a route from being activated. It can be used to check if a user is logged in, has the necessary permissions, or is allowed to access a route.

CanDeactivate: This guard is used to prevent a route from being deactivated. It can be used to check if a user is logged in, has the necessary permissions, or is allowed to access a route.

CanLoad: This guard is used to prevent a route from being loaded. It can be used to check if a user is logged in, has the necessary permissions, or is allowed to access a route.

Lazy loading and preloading strategies in Angular

Lazy loading is a strategy for loading content on demand, typically as the user scrolls down the page. This can improve performance by reducing the amount of data that needs to be downloaded, and can also improve the user experience by making content available as soon as it is needed.

Preloading is a strategy for loading content before it is needed, typically so that it is available as soon as the user navigates to the page. This can improve performance by reducing the amount of time the user has to wait for content to be downloaded, and can also improve the user experience by making sure that content is available when the user needs it.

Implementing nested routes and child routers in Angular

In Angular, a child router is a router-outlet directive that is placed inside another router-outlet. Child routers can be used to create nested routes, where each section of the website has its own router-outlet.

To implement nested routes, you first need to configure the parent router with a list of child routes. Each child route will have a path and a component. The path will be relative to the parent route.

For example, if the parent route is /products, then the child route for /products/:id will have the path ':id'.

The component for the child route will be rendered in the router-outlet of the parent component.

To configure the child routes, you need to use the children property of the route configuration object. The children property is an array of route configuration objects.

Each route configuration object in the children array will have a path and a component.

For example, if the parent route is /products, then the child route for /products/:id will have the path ':id' and the component ProductsComponent.

The router will match the paths of the child routes against the URL. If a match is found, the corresponding component will be rendered in the router-outlet of the parent component.

In the following example, the parent route is /products and the child routes are /products/:id and /products/:id/edit.

If the URL is /products/1, then the router will match the path ':id' of the child route and render the ProductsComponent.

If the URL is /products/1/edit, then the router will match the path ':id/edit' of the child route and render the ProductsEditComponent.

Chapter 5: Forms and Validation in Angular

Angular forms overview

The Angular forms module provides two ways to create forms in your application: template-driven and model-driven.

Template-driven forms are created using directives in the template. They are easy to use but they don't offer the full flexibility that model-driven forms offer.

Model-driven forms are created using the FormControl, FormGroup, and FormArray classes. They give you more control over how forms are created and how the data is validated.

Both types of forms can be used to create single-page or multi-page forms.

Single-page forms are forms that are displayed on one page. The data from the form is submitted all at once when the user clicks the submit button.

Multi-page forms are forms that are divided into multiple pages. The data from each page is submitted when the user clicks the next button.

Both types of forms can be used with either template-driven or model-driven forms.

Template-driven forms in Angular

A template-driven form is a form that is created using Angular template directives. These directives include things like ngModel and ngForm. With template-driven forms, the form's model is created by the template, and the form's validation is also handled by the template. This means that the form's data and validation logic are all contained within the template.

Template-driven forms are easy to use and quick to get up and running. However, they can be inflexible and difficult to debug. Additionally, because the form's model is created by the template, it can be difficult to unit test the form's logic.

Reactive forms and form validation in Angular

Reactive forms and form validation in Angular are two features that are often used together to create robust and user-friendly forms. Reactive forms provide a model-driven approach to form development, where the form's data is binded to a model, making it easy to track and validate changes. Form validation is the process of ensuring that user input is valid and correct before submitting the form. Angular provides a number of built-in validation directives, as well as an API for creating custom validation rules.

When using reactive forms, form controls can be created using the FormControl class. This class exposes a number of properties and methods that can be used to configure the control and track its value and validation status. The valueChanges observable can be used to monitor the control's value for changes, and the validity property can be used to check if the control is valid. To validate a control, Angular provides a number of built-in validation directives, such as the required directive. These directives can be used to add validation rules to form controls, and will automatically update the control's validity property when the user input is invalid.

Custom validation rules can be created using the Validators class. This class exposes a number of static methods that can be used to create custom validation functions. These functions can be used to validate the form control's value, and will return an error object if the value is invalid. The error object can be used to display an error message to the user.

Angular also provides a number of ways to customize the way form errors are displayed to the user. The ErrorStateMatcher class can be used to customize the way form control errors are displayed. The ng-messages directive can be used to display messages for specific form control errors. And the formGroup directive can be used to group form controls together, making it easier to display error messages for multiple controls at once.

Working with form controls and form groups in Angular

In Angular, form controls and form groups are two ways to create forms. Form controls are individual form elements, such as input, select, and textarea. Form groups are groups of form controls.

Both form controls and form groups can be created using the FormBuilder class. To create a form control, use the FormBuilder.control() method. To create a form group, use the FormBuilder.group() method.

Form controls and form groups can be used together to create more complex forms. To add a form control to a form group, use the FormGroup.addControl() method. To add a form group to a form group, use the FormGroup.addGroup() method.

Both form controls and form groups have a value property. The value property is an object that contains the values of the form controls in the form group. To get the value of a form control, use the FormControl.value property. To get the value of a form group, use the FormGroup.value property.

Both form controls and form groups have a setValue() method. The setValue() method sets the value of the form control or form group. The setValue() method takes an object that contains the new values of the form controls in the form group.

Both form controls and form groups have a patchValue() method. The patchValue() method sets the value of the form control or form group. The patchValue() method takes an object that contains the new values of the form controls in the form group. The patchValue() method only sets the values of the form controls that are specified in the object.

Both form controls and form groups have a reset() method. The reset() method resets the value of the form control or form group to its initial value.

Both form controls and form groups have a disabled property. The disabled property is a boolean value that determines whether the form control or form group is disabled. When a form control or form group is disabled, the form control or form group cannot be changed.

Both form controls and form groups have an errors property. The errors property is an object that contains the errors of the form control or form group. The errors object has two properties: the touched property and the pristine property.

The touched property is a boolean value that determines whether the form control or form group has been touched. A form control or form group is touched when the user interacts with the form control or form group.

The pristine property is a boolean value that determines whether the form control or form group is pristine. A form control or form group is pristine when the form control or form group has not been changed.

Custom form validators and error handling in Angular

Custom form validators and error handling can be implemented in Angular by creating a custom directive. This custom directive can then be used to validate the form and handle any errors that occur.

To create a custom form validator, you will first need to create a directive. This directive will contain the logic for your custom validation. Once you have created your directive, you will then need to register it with the form.

The following is an example of a custom form validator directive:

```
angular.module('myApp', [])
.directive('myCustomValidator', function() { return
{ require: 'ngModel', link: function(scope, element,
attrs, ngModel) { //Your validation logic goes here
} }; });
```

This directive can then be used to validate the form as follows:

```
<form name="myForm" my-custom-validator> ...
</form>
```

If there are any errors that occur during the validation process, they can be handled by using the $error object. This object contains information about all of the errors that have occurred.

For example, if you wanted to display an error message when the form is invalid, you could do the following:

```
<div ng-show="myForm.$error.myCustomValidator"> The form is invalid! </div>
```

The $error object can also be used to style the form elements that have caused an error. For example, if you wanted to add a red border to all of the invalid form elements, you could do the following:

```
<style> .ng-invalid { border: 1px solid red; } </style>
```

This will add a red border to all of the form elements that are invalid.

Chapter 6: HTTP Communication in Angular

Introduction to HTTP module in Angular

The HTTP module provides the basic functionality for sending and receiving data via the HTTP protocol. It can be used with the native HTTP client or with a third-party HTTP client library.

The HTTP module provides two methods for sending data: the request() method and the post() method. The request() method is used for GET requests, while the post() method is used for POST requests.

The HTTP module also provides a method for receiving data: the response() method. This method takes an HTTP response and returns an observable.

The HTTP module provides a number of options for configuring the request. These options can be passed to the request() or post() method.

The options object can contain the following properties:

method: The HTTP method to use for the request. The default is GET.

url: The URL to which the request will be sent.

headers: The headers to include in the request.

body: The body of the request.

params: The URL parameters to include in the request.

responseType: The response type. The default is text.

withCredentials: Whether or not to include credentials in the request. The default is false.

The HTTP module also provides a number of options for configuring the response. These options can be passed to the response() method.

The options object can contain the following properties:

observe: The type of events to observe. The default is events.

responseType: The response type. The default is text.

withCredentials: Whether or not to include credentials in the response. The default is false.

Sending GET, POST, PUT, and DELETE requests in Angular

GET, POST, PUT, and DELETE requests are all methods used to communicate with a web server. Angular is a framework that helps make these requests easier to work with.

GET requests are used to retrieve data from a server. This data is typically in the form of JSON or XML.

POST requests are used to send data to a server. This data is typically in the form of form data or JSON.

PUT requests are used to update data on a server. This data is typically in the form of JSON.

DELETE requests are used to delete data on a server. This data is typically in the form of JSON.

Handling request and response using observables in Angular

In Angular, an observable is a class that provides a way to produce and consume values over time. An observable can be used to create a stream of values, which can be subscribed to by one or more observers. When an observable produces a new value, it notifies its observers, and the observers can then consume the value.

Observables are used in Angular for handling asynchronous data, such as data that comes from a server. When a request is made to a server, an observable is used to represent the response from the server. The response from the server is delivered as a stream of values, which are then consumed by the observers.

Angular provides a number of ways to consume values from an observable. The most common way is to use the subscribe() method, which takes an observer as an argument. The observer can be a function, which will be called each time a new value is emitted from the observable. Alternatively, the observer can be an object with a next() method, which will be called each time a new value is emitted from the observable.

Once an observer has been registered with an observable, the observable will begin emitting values. The values will be delivered to the observer as they are received from the server. If the observable completes, meaning it has emitted all the values it is going to emit, the observer will be notified and the subscription will be unsubscribed.

If an error occurs while the observable is emitting values, the observer will be notified of the error and the subscription will be unsubscribed.

Interceptors and error handling in HTTP requests in Angular

Interceptors are a powerful way to handle HTTP requests in Angular. They provide a way to intercept HTTP requests and responses to transform or handle them in some way.

Error handling is a critical part of any HTTP request. Angular provides a way to handle errors via interceptors. When an error occurs, the interceptor can take action, such as logging the error or redirecting the user to a error page.

Interceptors can be used to handle a wide variety of HTTP requests, including errors. In this way, they provide a great deal of flexibility and power when it comes to handling HTTP requests in Angular.

Caching and authentication with HTTP requests in Angular

Caching can be used to improve the performance of an Angular application by storing the results of HTTP requests and serving them from the cache instead of making a new request each time. This can be especially useful for requests that are made frequently, such as requests for data that is used to populate a drop-down list.

Authentication can be used to protect sensitive data from being accessed by unauthorized users. Angular provides various mechanisms for implementing authentication, such as using the HTTP Basic authentication protocol or JSON Web Tokens.

Chapter 7: State Management with NgRx in Angular

Understanding state management and NgRx in Angular

State management is a process of managing the state of an application. The state of an application includes the data that is being used by the application, the UI state, the application logic, and the application state. NgRx is a library for Angular that helps to manage the state of an application. NgRx provides a set of tools that can be used to manage the state of an application. These tools include a reducer, a dispatcher, a selector, and an action creator. The reducer is responsible for handling the state of the application. The dispatcher is responsible for dispatching the actions to the reducer. The selector is responsible for selecting the data from the store. The action creator is responsible for creating the actions.

Setting up NgRx in Angular application can be done using the following steps:

1. Install the NgRx Store module using the following command:

npm install @ngrx/store

2. Import the StoreModule into your Angular AppModule:

import { StoreModule } from '@ngrx/store';

@NgModule({

imports: [

StoreModule.forRoot({})

]

})

export class AppModule {}

3. Add the StoreDevtoolsModule to your AppModule imports if you want to use the Redux DevTools:

```
import { StoreDevtoolsModule } from '@ngrx/store-devtools';

@NgModule({

imports: [

StoreModule.forRoot({}),

StoreDevtoolsModule.instrument({

maxAge: 25 //  Retains last 25 states

})

]

})

export class AppModule {}
```

4. Create your NgRx Action creators and Reducers.

5. Dispatch your NgRx Actions from your Angular components.

6. Select data from the NgRx Store using the NgRx StoreSelectors.

Actions

In Angular, actions are defined using the @ngrx/store/src/actions module. An action is a plain JavaScript object that contains a type property. The type property is a string that represents the type of action that has occurred. In addition to the type property, an action can also optionally include a payload property. The payload property is used to store any additional data that is associated with the action.

Reducers

In Angular, reducers are defined using the @ngrx/store/src/reducers module. A reducer is a pure function that takes the current state and an action, and returns a new state. The new state is calculated based on the type of action that was passed in.

Selectors

In Angular, selectors are defined using the @ngrx/store/src/selectors module. A selector is a function that takes the current state and returns a subset of that state. Selectors are used to retrieve specific data from the store.

Managing side effects with NgRx effects in Angular

There are several ways to manage side effects with NgRx effects in Angular. The easiest way is to use the provided NgRxEffectsModule. With this module, you can specify which effect should be run when an action is dispatched. For example, if you wanted to run an effect when the 'LOAD_USERS' action is dispatched, you would use the following code:

```
@NgModule({ imports: [
NgRxEffectsModule.forRoot([LoadUsers]) ],
providers: [LoadUsers] }) export class AppModule
{}
```

Now, whenever the 'LOAD_USERS' action is dispatched, the 'LoadUsers' effect will be run.

Another way to manage side effects is to use the '@Effect()' decorator. With this decorator, you can specify which action should trigger the effect. For example, if you wanted to run an effect when the 'LOAD_USERS' action is dispatched, you would use the following code:

```
@Effect() loadUsers$ = this.actions$.pipe(
ofType('LOAD_USERS'), switchMap(() =>
this.userService.loadUsers()), map((users: User[])
=> new LoadUsersSuccess(users)) );
```

Now, whenever the 'LOAD_USERS' action is dispatched, the 'loadUsers$' effect will be run.

There are many other ways to manage side effects with NgRx. For more information, please see the NgRx documentation.

Best practices and advanced concepts in NgRx in Angular

Best practices and advanced concepts in NgRx in Angular include:

1. Avoiding mutating state: State in NgRx should be treated as immutable. This means that you should never directly mutate state, but rather create new copies of state with the desired changes. This ensures that the state history is preserved and that different parts of the application can safely rely on the state.

2. Using selectors: Selectors are a powerful tool that can be used to efficiently query the state. They can be used to select a specific slice of state or to compute derived data from the state.

3. Normalizing state: In some cases, it may be beneficial to normalize the state. This means organizing the state in a way that makes it easy to query and update. For example, if you have a state that contains a list of items, you may want to normalize the state so that each item has its own unique identifier. This would make it easy to query specific items from the state and to update them without having to loop through the entire list.

4. Using reducer functions: Reducer functions are used to update the state. They take the current state and an action, and return a new state. It is important to keep reducer functions pure, meaning that they should not mutate the state or perform side effects.

5. Using action types: Action types are used to describe the actions that can be dispatched. They should be defined as constants so that they can be easily referenced throughout the application.

6. Using action creators: Action creators are functions that create actions. They should be used to encapsulate the logic for creating actions. This makes it easy to unit test the action creators and to change the action creator logic without having to change the code that dispatches the actions.

7. Using effects: Effects are used to perform side effects in response to actions. They should be used for tasks such as fetching data from an API or persisting data to a database.

8. Using NgRx Store Devtools: The NgRx Store Devtools is a powerful tool that can be used to debug and profile NgRx applications. It provides a time-traveling debugger that lets you see the state of the application at different points in time. It also provides a performance monitor that can be used to identify performance bottlenecks.

9. Using the NgRx Router Store: The NgRx Router Store is a library that provides bindings for NgRx and the Angular Router. It lets you easily dispatch actions when the router navigates. It also provides a way to select the current route state from the store.

10. Using immutable data structures: Immutable data structures should be used for the state. This ensures that the state cannot be directly mutated. It also makes it easier to use NgRx with React, as React relies on immutable data structures.

Chapter 8: Angular and RESTful APIs

Consuming RESTful APIs in Angular

There are various ways to consume RESTful APIs in Angular, but one of the most common ways is to use the HttpClient service. The HttpClient service is a built-in Angular service that provides various methods for making HTTP requests. To use the HttpClient service, you need to inject it into your component or service.

Once you have injected the HttpClient service, you can use its various methods to make HTTP requests. For example, the get() method makes a GET request, the post() method makes a POST request, and so on. Each method takes an URL and an optional options object as arguments. The options object allows you to specify the headers, body, and other options for the request.

Once you have made a request, the HttpClient service returns an observable. You can subscribe to this observable to get the response from the API. The observable emits a data event each time it receives a new piece of data from the API.

In addition to the HttpClient service, there are also various Angular libraries that make it easier to consume RESTful APIs. For example, the Angular HTTP library provides a higher-level API for making HTTP requests. The Angular Resource library provides a wrapper around the HttpClient service that makes it easier to work with RESTful APIs.

Working with RESTful API endpoints in Angular

In Angular, working with RESTful API endpoints is relatively simple. The $http service is provided by Angular and allows you to make HTTP requests to your API endpoint.

Assuming you have a RESTful API endpoint set up at http://example.com/api, you can make a GET request to retrieve data as follows:

$http.get('http://example.com/api/data').then(function(response) { // handle success });

To make a POST request, you can use the $http.post() method:

```
$http.post('http://example.com/api/data', { data:
'some data' }).then(function(response) { // handle
success });
```

If you need to make a PUT or DELETE request, you
can use the $http.put() or $http.delete() methods
respectively.

Making HTTP requests in Angular is simple and
straightforward. Once you have your API endpoint
set up, you can start making requests and handling
the responses in your Angular application.

Implementing pagination and filtering in Angular

Pagination and filtering are two common features
that are often required when working with data
from a REST API. In Angular, these can be
implemented using the built-in directives and
pipes.

The built-in directive for pagination is the ngForOf
directive. This directive can be used to render a list
of items from an array or an object. The directive

takes an input property called itemsPerPage which specifies the number of items to be rendered on each page. The directive also has an output property called pageChange which can be used to get the current page number.

The built-in pipe for filtering is the filter pipe. This pipe can be used to filter an array or an object based on a predicate function. The predicate function is passed two arguments: the value of the item and the index of the item. The function should return true if the item should be included in the filtered array, false otherwise.

To use the ngForOf directive, you first need to import the FormsModule from @angular/forms. You then need to add the directive to the template. The following is an example of how to use the ngForOf directive to render a list of items:

```
<ul>

<li *ngForOf="let item of items | paginate: {
itemsPerPage: 10, currentPage: page }">

{{ item }}

</li>

</ul>
```

To use the filter pipe, you first need to import the CommonModule from @angular/common. You then need to add the pipe to the template. The following is an example of how to use the filter pipe to filter an array of items:

```
<ul>

<li *ngForOf="let item of items | filter: { predicate: isItemVisible, index: i }">

{{ item }}

</li>

</ul>
```

The isItemVisible function is a predicate function that returns true if the item should be included in the filtered array, false otherwise. The index parameter is the index of the item in the array.

The following is an example of how to use the filter pipe to filter an object:

```
<ul>

<li *ngForOf="let item of items | filter: { predicate:
isItemVisible, key: 'name' }">

{{ item.name }}

</li>

</ul>
```

The isItemVisible function is a predicate function
that returns true if the item should be included in
the filtered object, false otherwise. The key
parameter is the name of the property to be
filtered on.

Error handling and retry strategies in Angular

In Angular, error handling and retry strategies can
be implemented in a number of ways. One way is
to use the $http service's error function. This
function takes a function as an argument that will
be called if an error occurs when making an HTTP
request. The function will be passed two
arguments: the first is an error object, and the
second is the HTTP response object.

Another way to handle errors is to use the $q service. This service provides a way to handle promises, which can be used to handle asynchronous operations such as HTTP requests. The $q service has a method called "catch" which takes a function as an argument. This function will be called if an error occurs when making an asynchronous operation. The function will be passed two arguments: the first is an error object, and the second is the data that was returned from the operation.

If you want to retry an operation if an error occurs, you can use the $q service's "retry" method. This method takes a function as an argument that will be called if an error occurs when making an asynchronous operation. The function will be passed three arguments: the first is an error object, the second is the number of times the operation has been retried, and the third is the data that was returned from the operation.

You can also use the $resource service to handle errors and retry strategies. The $resource service is a factory that creates a resource object that can be used to make HTTP requests. The resource object has a "catch" method that takes a function as an argument. This function will be called if an error occurs when making an HTTP request. The function will be passed two arguments: the first is an error object, and the second is the HTTP response object.

You can also use the $timeout service to handle errors and retry strategies. The $timeout service is a function that takes a function as an argument and returns a promise. The function will be called if an error occurs when making an asynchronous operation. The function will be passed two arguments: the first is an error object, and the second is the data that was returned from the operation.

Testing Angular services and HTTP requests

When testing Angular services and HTTP requests, there are a few key things to keep in mind. First, you will need to mock out the backend service or API that the Angular application is calling. This can be done with a library like Angular-mocks. Second, you will need to set up your test environment to run the Angular application. This can be done with a tool like Karma. Finally, you will need to write your tests. Some things to keep in mind when writing your tests include testing for correct HTTP status codes, testing the data that is returned from the API, and testing for error conditions.

Chapter 9: Unit Testing in Angular

Introduction to unit testing in Angular

In Angular, unit testing is performed using the Jasmine framework. Jasmine is a behavior-driven development framework for testing JavaScript code. It provides a way to write tests that are both easy to read and easy to maintain.

Angular also provides a number of tools for unit testing, including the Angular CLI and the karma test runner. The Angular CLI can be used to generate a boilerplate unit test file, which karma can then be used to execute.

Unit testing is an important part of the development process. It helps to ensure that code is working as expected and that new code does not break existing functionality. It also helps to identify bugs early on, before they become difficult to track down.

Angular's unit testing support and tools make it easy to get started with unit testing. In addition, there are a number of resources available online to help learn more about unit testing in Angular.

Setting up testing environment with Karma and Jasmine in Angular

In order to set up a testing environment with Karma and Jasmine in Angular, you will need to install both Karma and Jasmine. You can do this using the following commands:

```
npm install -g karma
npm install -g jasmine
```

Once both Karma and Jasmine are installed, you will need to create a karma.conf.js file in the root directory of your project. You can do this using the following command:

```
touch karma.conf.js
```

Inside the karma.conf.js file, you will need to add the following code:

```
module.exports = function(config) {
```

```javascript
config.set({

// base path that will be used to resolve all
patterns (eg. files, exclude)

basePath: '',

// frameworks to use

// available frameworks:
https://npmjs.org/browse/keyword/karma-
adapter

frameworks: ['jasmine'],

// list of files / patterns to load in the browser

files: [

'*.js'

],

// list of files to exclude

exclude: [

],

// preprocess matching files before serving them
to the browser

// available preprocessors:
https://npmjs.org/browse/keyword/karma-
preprocessor
```

```
preprocessors: {

},

// test results reporter to use

// possible values: 'dots', 'progress'

// available reporters:
https://npmjs.org/browse/keyword/karma-
reporter

reporters: ['progress'],

// web server port

port: 9876,

// enable / disable colors in the output (reporters
and logs)

colors: true,

// level of logging

// possible values: config.LOG_DISABLE ||
config.LOG_ERROR || config.LOG_WARN ||
config.LOG_INFO || config.LOG_DEBUG

logLevel: config.LOG_INFO,

// enable / disable watching file and executing
tests whenever any file changes

autoWatch: true,
```

```
// start these browsers

// available browser launchers:
https://npmjs.org/browse/keyword/karma-
launcher

browsers: ['Chrome'],

// Continuous Integration mode

// if true, Karma captures browsers, runs the tests
and exits

singleRun: false,

// Concurrency level

// how many browser should be started
simultaneous

concurrency: Infinity

})

}
```

Once the karma.conf.js file is set up, you can then
start Karma using the following command:

karma start karma.conf.js

Writing unit tests for components and services in Angular

There are many ways to write unit tests for components and services in Angular. One way is to use the Angular TestBed to create a testing module for each component or service. This module can then be used to inject the component or service into the test and run individual tests against it. Another way is to use a unit testing framework like Jasmine or Mocha to write unit tests that are run against the Angular code. These tests can be run in a browser or headless environment like Karma.

Testing asynchronous code and observables in Angular

When testing asynchronous code and observables in Angular, there are a few things to keep in mind. First, it is important to understand that observables are not immediately executed when they are subscribed to. Instead, they are executed when the observable is subscribed to, and the data is emitted asynchronously. This means that when testing observables, we need to use the async and fakeAsync utilities provided by Angular.

Second, we need to be aware of the difference between subscribing to an observable and subscribing to a promise. When we subscribe to an observable, we are actually setting up a subscription that will be executed when the observable emits data. This is different from subscribing to a promise, where the code inside the subscription will be executed immediately.

Finally, we need to be aware of the difference between unsubscribing from an observable and unsubscribing from a promise. When we unsubscribe from an observable, we are actually cancelling the subscription. This is different from unsubscribing from a promise, where we are simply ignoring the data that is emitted.

With these considerations in mind, let's take a look at how we can test asynchronous code and observables in Angular.

First, we need to import the async and fakeAsync utilities:

```
import { async, fakeAsync } from
'@angular/core/testing';
```

Next, we need to write a test that subscribes to an observable:

```
it('should subscribe to an observable',
fakeAsync(() => { const data = of('data'); let result;
data.subscribe(res => result = res); tick();
expect(result).toEqual('data'); }));
```

In this test, we create an observable with the of operator and subscribe to it. We then call the tick function to trigger the observable to emit its data. Finally, we assert that the data we received is correct.

Next, we need to write a test that unsubscribes from an observable:

```
it('should unsubscribe from an observable',
fakeAsync(() => { const data = of('data'); let result;
const subscription = data.subscribe(res => result =
res); subscription.unsubscribe(); tick();
expect(result).toEqual(undefined); }));
```

In this test, we create an observable and subscribe to it. We then unsubscribe from the observable and call the tick function. Finally, we assert that the data we received is undefined.

Finally, we need to write a test that subscribes to a promise:

```
it('should subscribe to a promise', fakeAsync(() =>
{ const data = Promise.resolve('data'); let result;
data.then(res => result = res); tick();
expect(result).toEqual('data'); }));
```

In this test, we create a promise and subscribe to it. We then call the tick function. Finally, we assert that the data we received is correct.

Code coverage and best practices for testing in Angular

Code coverage is a measure of how much of your code is being tested by your unit tests. The goal is to have a high code coverage so that you can be confident that your code is well-tested and has a high chance of being free of bugs.

There are a few different ways to measure code coverage, but one common way is to use a tool like Istanbul to generate a report. This report will show you which lines of code are covered by your tests and which are not.

Ideally, you want to aim for a high code coverage percentage. However, it is also important to make sure that your tests are covering the most important parts of your code. For example, it is often more important to have a test for a critical piece of functionality than a test for a less important edge case.

There are a few different best practices for unit testing in Angular that can help you write high-quality tests. First, it is important to write tests that are isolated from the implementation details of your component. This means that your tests should not rely on any implementation details that could change in the future.

Instead, your tests should focus on the public API of your component. This will make your tests more robust and less likely to break when the implementation details change.

Another best practice is to write tests that are easy to read and understand. This will make it easier to debug your tests if they do fail. Additionally, well-written tests can serve as documentation for your code and can help others understand how your component works.

Finally, it is important to run your tests regularly. This will help you catch any bugs that might be introduced into your code. Additionally, it can be helpful to run your tests on a continuous integration server so that they are run automatically every time you make a change to your code.

Chapter 10: Advanced Component Techniques in Angular

Dynamic component creation and rendering in Angular

In Angular, dynamic component creation and rendering refers to the ability to create and render components on the fly, as opposed to statically declaring them in advance. This can be useful in a number of situations, such as when you want to dynamically load a component based on user input, or when you want to create a component on the fly in response to some event.

To dynamically create and render a component in Angular, you first need to create a component factory. This can be done using the ComponentFactoryResolver service, which is provided by the Angular platform. Once you have a component factory, you can then use it to create a component instance and render it in any location within your application template.

Creating a component factory is a relatively simple process:

First, you need to import the ComponentFactoryResolver service from @angular/core :

```
import { ComponentFactoryResolver } from '@angular/core';
```

Next, you need to inject the ComponentFactoryResolver service into your component class:

```
constructor(private componentFactoryResolver: ComponentFactoryResolver) { }
```

Once you have injected the ComponentFactoryResolver service, you can then use it to resolve a component factory for any component type. For example, if you have a component called MyComponent , you can use the ComponentFactoryResolver to get a factory for it like so:

```
const componentFactory = this.componentFactoryResolver.resolveComponentFactory(MyComponent);
```

Once you have a component factory, you can then use it to create a component instance and render it in any location within your application template. For example, you could add the following to your component's template:

```
<div #container></div>
```

And then in your component class, you could use the component factory to create and render a MyComponent instance in the container div like so:

```
const componentRef = this.container.createComponent(componentFactory);
```

This would result in the following being rendered in the container div:

```
<my-component></my-component>
```

You can also pass input data to the dynamically-created component by using the component's input bindings. For example, if MyComponent has an input binding called name , you can set its value when creating the component instance like so:

```
componentRef.instance.name = 'John Smith';
```

This would result in the following being rendered in the container div:

```
<my-component name="John Smith"></my-component>
```

In addition to input bindings, you can also access the dynamically-created component's other properties and methods using the componentRef instance. For example, you could call a method on the component like so:

```
componentRef.instance.someMethod();
```

You can also destroy the dynamically-created component using the ComponentRef 's destroy() method:

```
componentRef.destroy();
```

This will remove the component from the DOM and clean up any associated resources.

Dynamic component creation and rendering can be a useful tool in a number of situations. It can be used to dynamically load a component based on user input, or to create a component on the fly in response to some event. It can also be used to provide a more flexible and powerful way to work with components in your Angular applications.

Component communication using input/output properties in Angular

Input/output properties are a way of passing data into and out of Angular components. They are declared using the @Input and @Output decorators.

Input properties are used to pass data into a component. They are declared using the @Input decorator.

Output properties are used to emit data out of a component. They are declared using the @Output decorator.

Input/output properties can be used to communicate between components that are parent and child, or sibling components.

ViewChild and ContentChild are decorators in
Angular that can be used to access child
components in a parent component.

ViewChild allows a parent component to access a
child component by its selector. For example, if a
parent component has a child component with the
selector "#myChild", the ViewChild decorator can
be used to access that child component.

ContentChild works similarly to ViewChild, but
instead of using a child component's selector, it
uses the content of the child component. This is
useful for accessing embedded content in a child
component, such as an ng-template.

**There are two change detection strategies in
Angular:**

1) Default change detection

2) OnPush change detection

Default change detection is the default strategy used by Angular. It checks for changes in the component and its child components every time there is an event, such as a user input.

OnPush change detection is a more optimized strategy that only checks for changes in the component when an input event occurs. This can improve performance in large applications where there are many components.

Creating reusable components and component libraries in Angular

Angular allows us to create reusable components and component libraries. This is extremely helpful when building large-scale applications, as it allows us to break our code down into smaller, more manageable pieces.

Creating a reusable component is simple. First, we create a new Angular component using the Angular CLI. For example, we could create a new component called "my-component" like so:

ng generate component my-component

This will create a new folder called "my-component" in our project, containing the necessary files for our new component.

Once our component is generated, we can add it to any other Angular component as a child. For example, we could add it to the "app" component like so:

Now, our "my-component" component will be rendered whenever the "app" component is rendered.

We can also create a component library, which is simply a collection of Angular components that can be reused in multiple projects. To do this, we first create a new Angular project using the Angular CLI. For example, we could create a new project called "my-library" like so:

ng new my-library

This will create a new folder called "my-library" in our project, containing the necessary files for our new library.

Next, we generate our components within our new library. For example, we could generate a new component called "my-component" like so:

ng generate component my-component

This will create a new folder called "my-component" in our library, containing the necessary files for our new component.

Now, we can build our library using the Angular CLI. For example, we could build our library for production like so:

ng build my-library --prod

This will output our built library into the "dist" folder.

Finally, we can publish our library to a repository such as npm. Doing so will allow others to install and use our library in their own Angular projects.

Chapter 11: Internationalization and Localization in Angular

Introduction to internationalization and localization in Angular

One of the most important aspects of creating applications that can be used by people around the world is to make sure that they can be easily translated and localized for different languages and regions. This process is known as internationalization and localization, and it is something that Angular is very well suited for.

There are two main approaches that can be taken when internationalizing an Angular application:

1. Use the built-in i18n tooling that Angular provides. This approach is suitable for applications that are not too complex and do not need to support a large number of languages.

2. Use a third-party library such as ngx-translate. This approach is more suitable for large applications or those that need to support a large number of languages.

Whichever approach is taken, there are a few key things to keep in mind:

1. All text strings in the application should be externalized so that they can be easily translated.

2. The application should be designed in a way that makes it easy to switch between different languages.

3. All date, time, and number formats should be configurable so that they can be displayed correctly in different regions.

4. Any images or other media should be provided in a format that can be easily translated.

5. The application should be tested in different languages and regions to make sure that everything works as expected.

Configuring multiple languages in Angular

When configuring multiple languages in Angular, there are two main steps:

1. Configuring the Angular application itself to support multiple languages. This can be done by providing a configuration object to the angular.configure method. This object should

contain a key-value pair for each language supported, with the key being the language code and the value being an object containing localization information for that language.

2. Configuring the individual components in your application to support multiple languages. This can be done by providing a locale id to the component's constructor. The locale id should be a string containing the language code for the language you wish to support.

For more information on configuring Angular for multiple languages, see the Angular documentation.

Implementing translations with ngx-translate in Angular

In order to use ngx-translate in your Angular project, you will need to install the module via npm:

```
$ npm install @ngx-translate/core --save
```

Once the module is installed, you can import it into your root NgModule:

```
import { NgModule } from '@angular/core'; import
{ BrowserModule } from '@angular/platform-
browser'; import { AppComponent } from
'./app.component'; // import the module import {
TranslateModule } from '@ngx-translate/core';
@NgModule({ declarations: [ AppComponent ],
imports: [ BrowserModule, // include the module
in your AppModule imports
TranslateModule.forRoot() ], bootstrap: [
AppComponent ] }) export class AppModule { }
```

After the module is imported, you can then define a set of translations to use in your application. For example, you could create a file called src/assets/i18n/en.json with the following contents:

```
{ "HELLO": "Hello", "GOODBYE": "Goodbye" }
```

And then another file for a different language, src/assets/i18n/es.json:

```
{ "HELLO": "Hola", "GOODBYE": "Adiós" }
```

Once you have defined your translations, you can then use them in your component templates using the translate pipe:

```
<p>{{ 'HELLO' | translate }}</p> <p>{{ 'GOODBYE' | translate }}</p>
```

If you want to dynamically change the language that is being used, you can inject the TranslateService into your component and call the use() method:

```
import { Component } from '@angular/core';
import { TranslateService } from '@ngx-translate/core'; @Component({ selector: 'app-root', templateUrl: './app.component.html', styleUrls: ['./app.component.css'] }) export class AppComponent { constructor(private translate: TranslateService) { } changeLanguage(language: string) { this.translate.use(language); } }
```

And then in your template, you can bind the changeLanguage() method to a language selector:

```
<select
(change)="changeLanguage($event.target.value)">
<option value="en">English</option> <option
value="es">Spanish</option> </select>
```

Now when the user changes the language, the corresponding translations will be used in the template.

Date, number, and currency formatting in Angular

The date, number, and currency formatting in Angular are all based on the Unicode CLDR (Common Locale Data Repository) specification. The CLDR is a collection of data that provides standards for date, number, and currency formatting across different locales.

Angular provides pipes for date, number, and currency formatting that use the CLDR standards.

The date pipe formats dates according to the specified locale, and the number and currency pipes format numbers and currencies according to the specified locale.

To format a date, use the date pipe. The date pipe takes a Date object or a string as an input and formats it according to the specified locale.

To format a number, use the number pipe. The number pipe takes a number as an input and formats it according to the specified locale.

To format a currency, use the currency pipe. The currency pipe takes a number as an input and formats it as a currency according to the specified locale.

Best practices for building multilingual applications in Angular

There are a few different ways to approach building multilingual applications in Angular, and the best approach may vary depending on the specific requirements of the application. However, in general, the following guidelines may be useful when building multilingual applications in Angular:

1. Use the built-in Angular i18n tools for handling translations.

2. Keep the application structure simple and modular, so that it is easy to add or remove languages as needed.

3. Use language-specific folders for storing translations, so that it is clear which language each file belongs to.

4. Use a consistent naming convention for translation keys, so that it is easy to find the correct keys when translating.

5. Use placeholder values for dynamic content, so that the same translation can be used in multiple places.

6. Test the application with multiple languages to ensure that all functionality works as expected.

Chapter 12: Deployment and Optimization in Angular

Building and packaging Angular application for production

When building an Angular application for production, it is important to consider the size and performance of the application. The Angular compiler can help with this by creating smaller bundles that are faster to load.

It is also important to minify and uglify the code to reduce the size of the bundles. The Angular CLI can help with this as well.

Finally, it is important to gzip the bundles to reduce the size even further. This can be done with a third-party tool such as the Angular CLI.

Performance optimization techniques in Angular

:

- Ahead-of-time (AOT) compilation: This technique pre-compiles Angular HTML and

CSS templates at build time, which can significantly improve the performance of your app.

- Lazy loading: This technique loads Angular modules on demand as the user navigates to different parts of your app. Lazy loading can improve the startup performance of your app by loading only the modules that are needed at the initial state.
- Tree shaking: This technique removes unused code from your Angular modules to improve the performance of your app.
- Minification: This technique minifies your Angular code to reduce the size of your app and improve its performance.
- Bundling: This technique bundles your Angular modules into a single file to reduce the number of HTTP requests and improve the performance of your app.

Tree shaking and code minification in Angular

Angular Pro has two features that can help optimize your application for deployment: tree shaking and code minification.

Tree shaking is a way of removing unused code from your application. This can be used to remove unused code that is included in third-party libraries, for example. Code minification is a way of reducing the size of your code by making it more compact. This can make your application load faster and use less bandwidth.

Lazy loading and optimizing bundle size in Angular

Lazy loading is a technique in Angular that allows you to load JavaScript components asynchronously when a specific route is activated. This can be used to improve the performance of your Angular application by loading only the components that are required for the current route, and then loading additional components as needed.

To optimize the bundle size of your Angular application, you can use the Angular CLI to generate a production build. This will minify and uglify your JavaScript code, which will reduce the size of your bundle. You can also use the Angular CLI to Ahead of Time (AOT) compile your application, which will further reduce the size of your bundle.

Continuous integration and deployment strategies in Angular

There are a few different ways to set up continuous integration and deployment (CI/CD) for an Angular application. One popular way is to use a tool like Jenkins, which can be configured to automatically build and deploy your application whenever new code is pushed to your repository.

Another popular option is to use a cloud-based CI/CD service like Travis CI or CircleCI. These services make it easy to set up a CI/CD pipeline for your Angular application with just a few clicks.

Once you have your CI/CD pipeline set up, you can start thinking about how you want to deploy your Angular application. One option is to host your application on a platform like Heroku or AWS.

Another option is to use a static site hosting service like Netlify or Surge. These services make it easy to deploy your Angular application as a static site, which can be easily scaled and is very cost-effective.

Finally, you can also choose to deploy your Angular application locally. This is a good option if you want to have complete control over your application and don't want to rely on a third-party service.

No matter which option you choose, the important thing is to have a plan for how you will deploy your Angular application. By having a CI/CD pipeline in place, you can make sure that your application is always up-to-date and can be easily deployed to any environment.

www.ingramcontent.com/pod-product-compliance
Lightning Source LLC
LaVergne TN
LVHW051709050326
832903LV00032B/4107